Work Work Work: The Assistant's Guide to
Getting Even More Work Done
(Yeah Right)

By
PennyLee

© 2006 by Fire Signs Inc.
All rights reserved.

ISBN 978-0-6151-3611-0
LCCN

Printed in the United States of America.

1st edition Copyright 2000
2nd edition Copyright 2006

Table of Contents

INTRODUCTION 5
   Diary #1 (The Novice) 7
   DARN BOSS 11
   DON'T YOU HATE IT WHEN… 11
   BUT IT WASN'T MY FAULT!!! 11

DARN BOSS 12

DON'T YOU HATE IT WHEN… 13

BUT IT'S NOT MY FAULT 15

THE NERVE 16

HOW LAZY IS YOUR BOSS?? 17
   Secret Legion of Assistants Versus their Evil Superiors 18
   S.L.A.V.E.S.= Secret Legion of Assistants Versus their Evil Superiors 19

THINGS MY BOSS DOES THAT I JUST DON'T UNDERSTAND 30
   THINGS THAT TURN YOUR GOOD DAY BAD 32

THINGS THAT TURN A GOOD DAY BAD… 33

UNINVITED GUEST AT THE WORK PLACE 35

THE EXPENSE REPORT FROM HELL 38
   ROLES ASSISTANTS PLAY 40

ROLES ASSISTANTS PLAY 41

ROLES YOUR BOSS WOULD ASK YOU TO PLAY IF SHE COULD GET AWAY WITH IT 49
   JUST CALL ME MANDO THE MAGNIFICENT 51

JUST CALL ME MANDO THE MAGNIFICENT 52
   YOU KNOW YOU'RE STRESSED WHEN… 55

YOU KNOW YOU'RE STRESSED WHEN… 56
   YOU KNOW YOU'RE A CHEESY ASSISTANT WHEN… 60

YOU KNOW YOU'RE A CHEESY ASSISTANT WHEN…	**61**
OOPS	**63**
PROBLEM…SOLUTION	64
PROBLEM…SOLUTION	**65**
MISTAKES ASSISTANTS MAKE…	68
MISTAKES ASSISTANTS MAKE…	**69**
THE DIARY PART II	71
(THE VETERAN)	71
THE DIARY PART II (THE VETERAN)	**72**
QUOTES	**84**
EPILOGUE	85
EPILOGUE	**86**

INTRODUCTION

"Assistant". The dictionary defines the word assistant as a helper. Subordinate. Nowhere does it define an assistant as a "mother" or "indentured servant."

We started writing this book as an outlet. We would call each other daily at work with one amazing story after another. "Let me tell you what happened today..."or "Oh My God! You'll never believe this..." were usual preludes to some unbelievable scenarios. We then started asking other assistants to tell us some of their stories and we started documenting them.

Once we accumulated what seemed like a small mountain of teeth grinding incidents, we realized what we had: a book. Not a novel, not a life's work, but a book that may be of value to someone besides ourselves. Someone could use it as a guide, so to speak- How to survive in the wonderful world of assisting, or maybe a self-improvement book- "How to become a better assistant". It could possibly be used by high school counselors as a motivator for higher education- "If you don't pass that algebra class this might be you." But for us, this book meets the ultimate purpose: a way to VENT! VENT! VENT! We figured if one assistant could get a smile out of this book and realize they are not crazy, if they can find comfort in the fact that there are others out there feeling their pain, then our work is done. We have totally unselfish reasons for doing this.

Now, this book is primarily written for the assistant, hence the size (easy to hide in the bottom drawer of your desk to be pulled out when one is in desperate need of some comic relief) the title (we knew that if we put the word "work" on the cover your boss would never think to open it) the cover (the black and white will easily blend into all those meaningless memos on your desk) and the simple wording (with all the reading and thinking you have to do, the last thing we want to do is make you have to look up any big words). Smart huh? However, after countless test readings we've found that others have also found enjoyment in this book just because they could relate to some of the stupidity and incompetence that they, too, must put up with in the workplace. Now go ahead, kick back and read on. It's set it up so you can open to almost any page in case you are too busy to read straight through. We hope you enjoy it, and remember-WE FEEL YOUR FRUSTRATION!!!!!!!!!!!!!!!!!!!!!!!!!!!!!!
PennyLee

Diary #1 (The Novice)

Today I have been given the official word that I got the job as an "ASSISTANT", in a very fine company. For the longest I thought I knew and understood the meaning of the word "Assistant". Well, let's just say I found out the hard way that the very same word "Assistant" takes on a whole new meaning every single day.

Today is my first day on the job and so far I feel like bacteria on a film slide, being magnified a million times over. It's very obvious that I am the new person on the job by my wide eye doe-like expression and huge, yet nervous, fake smile. It appears that everyone knows each other, and is very comfortable in their positions. As I desperately scope the office trying to pick up on the different personalities ranging from "The Company Witch" to "The Company Loser" I focus on my ace in the hole, A.K.A., "The Perfect Assistant". Little does this person know that I will milk her for all information I need until she curses me out and beats me with a silly stick. She should be extremely happy that there's only one of me lurking around this baby.

I sit at my desk and silently pray, to the highest power imaginable that my boss is going to be someone reasonable. Someone I can work with. While I'm praying, I'm interrupted by three simultaneously ringing phone lines. I nervously snatch one line hoping the caller will hang up. No such luck, instead they decide to inquire about information on a certain project that I am clueless about since it is my first day on the job. The other two lines are still ringing. I now place the first caller on hold as I grab the second line. I look over at the third line and I'm in luck, they decided to hang up or at least I think they did until I notice there is a message light. Uh oh, I haven't learned how to check the voice mail yet. I end up clearing both calls and proceed to sneak off to the "Perfect Assistant" to assist me in retrieving the message. As I'm trying to be discreet about asking for her assistance, she responds to me in the loudest tone possible, so everyone in the office becomes aware of the fact that I don't know what I'm doing. On the outside I humble myself and thank her for helping me, but on the inside I picture myself as a throat surgeon removing her voice box and flushing it down the toilet.

The day goes on with more silent prayers of pleading and even more annoying calls. One thing that really bothers me is when I greet a caller by stating my boss' name only to have them turn around and ask me whose office they are calling. When this happens, my first thought is "Idiot Caller". Then reality kicks in and I realize that I'm getting paid to repeat myself to people who don't know how to listen. What's more; this could be the "Very Important Call" my boss has been expecting. I soon learn that with my boss, all calls would be categorized as such, even the one from her manicurist informing her that the color nail polish she requested has arrived. Speaking of my boss, she has just arrived, gotta go.

DARN BOSS

DON'T YOU HATE IT WHEN...?

BUT IT WASN'T MY FAULT!!!

DARN BOSS

The worst thing a boss can say to you is "Just do whatever you want" "It's up to you" or "It doesn't matter", especially when asking you to pick out a gift for a very important client.

What usually happens is that you pick out a gift, send it, and then find out your boss hates it. For example, I was supposed to send someone a thank you basket. I asked my boss specifically what he wanted in it, to which he replied, "It doesn't matter, it is up to you." So with a price range in mind, I ordered a very nice, expensive gourmet food basket with smoked ham, olives, cheese and an assortment of gourmet meats. It sounded great to me. Well the next day having completed my task, I went back to my boss with a victorious grin, gleefully reporting that the basket had been sent and all was taken care of. When asked what kind of basket was sent I proudly exclaimed, "A GOURMET MEAT BASKET!" My boss then gave me a look of total disgust and said, "I told you he was a vegetarian!!"

AAARRRRRGGGHHHHHHHH!!!!!!!!!

DON'T YOU HATE IT WHEN...?

- ❖ Your boss tells you to hold all of his calls- NO MATTER WHAT! Then screams his bloody head off later in the day when he gets a message that you didn't put a call through to him from his golf partner.

- ❖ You try to give your boss directions for her lunch date. She insists that she doesn't need them. She's been there a thousand times she says. Then when you are busy doing a million other things, your boss calls back and asks for the directions. Of course, by now you've thrown them away since she told you she didn't need them. You then have to scramble around like a dummy turning over every little sticky note on your desk to find them.

❖ Your boss yells at you in that rude condescending tone that you would not even tolerate from your own birth mother.

❖ You change everyone's calendar to show that the 4:00pm meeting has been changed to 10:00am, and your stupid boss, who can always find time to check her social calendar, but evidently not her office calendar is the only one who misses the meeting. Guess who gets the blame?

BUT IT'S NOT MY FAULT

Joe calls your boss and it's urgent that he talks to him. Of course your boss is somewhere he should not be, doing something totally non-work related. So you make up a lame excuse and put Joe on hold. You search high and low and finally contact your boss. After some persuading he agrees to take the call. (Remember this is a call that needs his immediate attention and will benefit him, so it's not like he's doing Joe a favor). Anyway, while trying to reach your boss you were periodically checking back with Joe using the old favorites- "just one more second", "he'll be right with you" and "one moment please". Well, as you finally put your boss on hold, press the conference button and reach to take Joe off hold and begin to pat yourself on the back, guess what happens? Joe hangs up, and of course your boss is ticked. Not only have you disturbed his goofing off, but you've disconnected his *urgent* call from Joe. Yeah right! Like you could force Joe to wait on hold forever. Jeez!!

THE NERVE

Here are ways in which your boss likes to prove to you that her life is more important than yours:

You pick up your two kids from daycare at 6:30pm every day. You get off at 6:00pm. You've always gotten off at 6pm. The assistant before you got off at 6pm, yet your boss waits until 5:35pm to ask you to run stupid errands all the way across town. Even when she knows the daycare is prone to charge about $1000 for every 15 minutes you are late (well maybe not a $1000, but seeing how little you get paid any extra money that has to come out of your pocket seems like it's going to bankrupt you). You have mentioned to your boss several times and dropped millions of hints about the situation, yet she still refuses to get the picture. Your kid's daycare workers now give you the evil eye (you know the same one you give to your boss) and wait patiently—ready to take your extra money—for you to arrive huffing, puffing and full of apologies.

HOW LAZY IS YOUR BOSS??

My boss is so lazy…

- ❖ He calls me from his car to have me connect him to his best friend whose phone number is on his speed dial in his car.

- ❖ On a particular occasion I was faxed at the office by my boss a sixty page document from his location only to have me turn around and fax it to the intended recipient.

- ❖ I gave her a copy of her calendar only to have her lose it and then take my original and lose that as well. Then, not even one minute later I'm asked what her week looks like.

- ❖ I feel like dying a million deaths when his friends call and ask me for the phone numbers, addresses and cross streets to restaurants that I have never heard of before. I say loudly (while hoping they catch on) that I will call 411 and get this information for them.

Secret Legion of Assistants Versus their Evil Superiors

S.L.A.V.E.S. = Secret Legion of Assistants Versus their Evil Superiors

Secret hand shake- When members greet one another, they put their hands in the shape of a gun (you know, the second finger pointing out and the thumb pointing up) and aim it toward their heads then aim it outwards like their saying, "I'm either going to shoot her or myself, her or myself")

Top secret meeting days- The 2nd Sunday of the 5th month that has an "A" in it.

To be initiated:

Verbal jump in- 10 other assistants meet you in the coffee break room after dark. They line up five on each side and you have to go down the line and take their abuse. But unlike the physical jump-ins, in which the new member is hit, kicked and spit upon, the verbal jump-in consists of much, much more. Each assistant yells insane orders to you 20 at a time with no clarification. They berate and degrade you all the while smiling in your face. They have also been known to shout out smart aleck comments and insults and dare you to say something back.

<u>Mandatory sabotage</u>- The candidate is forced to purposely blow a major deal for his boss.

Pledge of Allegiance
We pledge allegiance to the Flag, of the United S.L.A.V.E.S. of America. And to all of its members, who take a stand, we're one nation under God; with intelligence and dignity after all.

Motto
No arguing amongst one another (Save all energy to direct hatred toward the bosses)

Cheer
2-4-6-8, who do we really hate? Our bosses, our bosses, boo bosses!

Monthly Newsletter

Agenda How to ruin your boss' career.
Your boss- Friend or Foe
How to blackmail your boss: A to Z guide to payback

Loathed assistant of the month- the office kiss up who is banned nationally from all S.L.A.V.E. chapters.

Hated boss of the month- qualifications: Not only gets on your nerves, but has gotten on the nerves of at least three other assistants in the last 30 days.

Classifieds
Job openings: Attention all S.L.A.V.E.S.:
For all those interested and qualified. As of tomorrow there will be an immediate opening at Peaches and Bean Inc. My big idiot boss has gotten on my last nerve. So I am quitting. Qualities needed: Must have low, low self-esteem, no back bone and must be very stupid (you have to be to put up with him). You can fax your resume or come in and say hi while I'm cursing him out and packing my stuff. Good luck.

Hey Join S.L.A.V.E.S. we have wonderful benefits!

Benefits:

Online service

This site is only for S.L.A.V.E.S. members. It is extremely useful and provides different services. Our website is full of excuses for absentees, tardiness, why that package was sent late, and a bonus, seniority package that comes fully equipped with over 10,000 excuses for any occasion.

Dry Cleaning

Special dry cleaning discount services that you use when you are at your boss' house and spill something on one her valuables. Just call the 8-digit number and they'll rush over, clean the items and give you back your sanity, which you lost while stressing over what just happened.

Medical Insurance

This insurance only covers job related injuries. You know migraines that come about from having to do the work of three people on one person's salary.

Arthritis
This, of course is a condition which you have developed over a span of one week from carrying her giant coffee mugs back and forth for refills, the constant opening of her diet sodas, and the famous curling your fingers to form a fist which you would like to use on her.

Acne
Caused by stressing over which would be a wiser career move:
- ❖ Getting kicked out of your apartment, having your car repossessed, moving back home with your "I told you so, parents", or
- ❖ Staying on the job.

Hunchback
This is caused by constantly bending over your computer screen while you send S.O.S. e-mail messages to the person in the cubical next to you hoping they will call for real help.

Scratch Therapy
To ease the pain from when you dig your finger nails into the palm of your hands while making a fist. Keep in mind this fist is

the same fist you would use to sock her, but then quickly realized you would probably get fired for doing so.

Hair Transplanting
To be used to put back the hair you've pulled out of your head while contemplating slapping everyone in the office.

Chap Stick for Life
To ease your cracked and dried lips from all the butt kissing which came about only after one day on the job.

Paper Shredder
For all the times you were used as the human paper shredder to tear up the important memos that the big boss is not supposed to get a copy of.

Witness Protection Program
This will allow you protection to move and change your identity once you've gone to the big boss to turn in your boss when you just can't take it anymore.

Authentic Laugh Re-installation
You've conditioned yourself so well to belt out fake laughs at your boss' bad jokes that the only way you can recapture your original laugh is to have this procedure.

Eye Glasses
Which you never thought you would need seeing that you started the job with 20/20 vision but are now standing at 20/2. Why? You strain your eyesight everyday trying to read your boss' kindergarten handwriting. You're also now cross-eyed from giving your boss the evil eye all the time or from rolling your eyes way back in your head whenever he comes up with the same idea you had yesterday.

The Secret Toll Free 922 Number (Instead of 911)
This is only to be used under dire circumstances. You know, right when you've assembled 200 paper clips into an automatic weapon that you will try to use to kill your boss. When you call the 922 number a retired assistant who has put it in, at the minimum 35 years of service to over 100 crazy bosses will answer the phone and calm you down. She'll tell you to push 1 or 2. Number 1 is for comic relief. You tell them your boss' first name and three negative adjectives and they make funny jokes about your boss for a good 4 minutes. If you push button 2, you'll get the helper. They'll say things like, "It's okay, don't kill her, she doesn't know better. Just let it go."

Unlimited Supply of Bengay
To ease your arthritis, which you developed over only a two day period with your boss. This came about from standing behind your boss while she's sitting in her big executive chair and you are leaning over her shoulders in the "I'm Gonna Choke You" stance.

Guaranteed A Position As A World Renowned Psychic for 800 and 900 Hotline Numbers
All the times you've had to read between the lines, assume you know what your boss is talking about, and guess who the caller is that refuses to state their name. Yes all of the above automatically qualifies you for this position and you get paid more money for doing it this time around.

New Pair of Tennis Shoes Every Week
You are given a new pair of tennis shoes every week for all the times you have to run down to your boss' car to hand her the important file she forgot while rushing to her car to make her spa appointment.

Endless Ice Packs
The endless ice packs comes in handy when you want to punch your boss in the mouth, but instead you walk away and punch a hole

in the down stairs parking garage wall. You then go to the freezer to retrieve that bad boy and place it on that newly busted fist.

Classes on "How To Lie"
These classes come in handy when you notice your boss wearing something even your grandmother wouldn't be caught dead in and she turns and asks how she looks.
- A. Do you tell her the truth and lose your job, or
- B. Lie like you've never lied before and keep your job while making her happy?

Tongue Reconstructive Surgery
For all the times you bite your tongue and in the process save your job. This comes about when you are on the brink of telling your boss just what she can kiss.

Neck Brace
For the times when you approach your boss with your well deserved request for a day off some time in the near future. As you're speaking, he tilts his head to the side while sucking on his rotten teeth with a dazed look of "how dare you ask me this question knowing good and well I've only taken four vacations so far this year". But before the obvious "NO" is given to you, for some

reason your head is now tilted to the side just like your boss'. But, this is not out of mockery of him, but rather out of hope that today might be the day this cold man might actually use his heart and grant you the time off. This doesn't happen and so your head tilting is now one of depression and your neck brace will be utilized to help correct your poor posture once again.

Relief Pitcher
You know how in baseball there is a relief pitcher; someone to step in when the pitcher is just so exhausted he can't go on. Well if you join S.L.A.V.E.S. one of the benefits we provide you with is a relief dummy. This life-like dummy is made from a mold of your body so he looks just like you. Here's how he works: When you are at your absolute limit and you cannot type or file one more item you push a button that has been secretly installed under your chair by our S.L.A.V.E.S. technician. This will automatically pop the dummy out of its secret compartment. Now the dummy is equipped with a super expensive hair implant that has been matched exactly to your own hair texture so that it looks like you from the back. And since your lazy boss never comes completely out of her office to yell her demands anyway, she'll never know

whether it's you or not. You can then leave the office for two or three hours to run personal errands and get that massage you've been needing forever.

THINGS MY BOSS DOES THAT I JUST DON'T UNDERSTAND

❖ A person left my boss a voicemail message stating that it's okay for her to call them tomorrow. My boss then turns around and asks me to call the person back the very same day to let them know she not only received the message, but will call them tomorrow; as if that wasn't understood in the message that the caller left.

❖ Leaving the office five minutes before his appointment which is on the other side of town and then gets mad because the person refuses to see him even though he's about an hour late.

❖ Telling me to get someone on the line while he is still on the first call only to have the second caller hang up because he took too long to get on the line. My boss then questions me in disbelief as to why the person hung up.

❖ Calling me on his cell with the "Very Important Dictated Memo" while going through a long tunnel knowing good and well that we will be disconnected. Then he calls back and asks me to read back what he just dictated.

❖ Wanting his expense check approved, signed, cut, and ready for deposit an hour after it was turned in to the accounting department from hell.

❖ Telling me to call the hippest restaurant of the moment for a same day reservation. I humor my boss and do as he says. While speaking to the reservationist, I'm instructed by my boss to state clearly our company's name, my boss' title, and to which celebrity he has frequented their restaurant with in the past. Of course these people could careless about who or what my boss is and I can now hear cricket and owl sounds as I give them my info. They are so not impressed and of course, they tell me they're totally booked. Now, how do I explain this to "His Royal Highness"?

THINGS THAT TURN YOUR GOOD DAY BAD

THINGS THAT TURN A GOOD DAY BAD...

Getting busted:

When you are on the phone laughing and joking with your friend; your boss calls on line 2 from her office and asks what you are doing. At this time your friend is on line 1 holding and you are silently telling your boss to get the hell off the phone so you can get back to the juicy gossip. You then tell your boss that you have been working on that big memo for her. As you are explaining how hard and diligently you've been working, the phone buzzes to remind you that you have someone on hold (of course you want to die because your boss heard the buzz too and she now knows you're on the phone). When she asks who you are talking to, you get ready to make up some elaborate lie when she (assuming the call is for her) hangs up on you, picks up the phone and listens to your friend laughing and giggling about some corny joke she just told you. Your boss gets off the phone with a disgusted look on her face and you quickly get on the phone and tell your friend in an embarrassing tone that you'll call her back.

UNINVITED GUEST AT THE WORK PLACE

There's nothing worse than uninvited guests at the job. This type of stuff can either make or break your reputation at work.

- ❖ Former high school classmates who forgot that carrying a can of beer with a straw in it while dressed alike is no longer cute. But was it ever?

- ❖ People you met while at a social function that were rude and loud but somehow able to track you down even though you never gave them your information.

- ❖ Loud and grammatically challenged friends.

- ❖ The person whose numerous phone calls you never return.

❖ The money-hungry-will-do anything-to-get-a-man girlfriend, who is aware of the major company you work for and the financial status of your male co-workers.

❖ Your boss' lover who feels she has a right to drop by even when she's told the wife is in with the boss.

❖ The alcoholic friend.

❖ People you owe money.

❖ The ex-boyfriend who just can't seem to get it in his head that IT'S OVER!!

❖ Friends with bad body odor.

❖ A child support representative with your subpoena.

❖ Scorned lovers.

❖ Confrontational baby's mama.

❖ Over coordinating aunt and uncle.

- ❖ The girlfriend who still wears black lip liner and three inch curved fingernails with rainbow airbrush.

- ❖ The infamous friend that just got out of jail and wants a hook-up with a job starting at top salary.

- ❖ Close talker who feels the need to be exactly in your face in order for you to understand what they are telling you.

- ❖ The office comedian with really bad redundant jokes who doesn't leave you alone until you laugh at one of them.

- ❖ The friend that always wants a favor but never has anything of any value to give you in return.

- ❖ The one person who "just doesn't get it."

THE EXPENSE REPORT FROM HELL

Here's another thing that can turn a good day bad. We are all aware that with each month comes an expense report. With each expense report comes the thought of suicide or premeditated murder and sometimes, both. Here's a list of things that come along with doing a monthly expense report:

- ❖ Trying to make up a date for receipts that have no dates listed on them.

- ❖ Making up names of people who were clearly out of town when the supposed engagement took place but putting their names on the receipt helps to validate it.

- ❖ Having people appear to be connected to a particular project even though another company is already in development with that particular project.

- ❖ Reading receipts that have grease and water stains on them with blurred figures of what should actually be numbers.

- ❖ Exaggerating the tips on the bill as well as the parking fee in order for your boss to receive a bigger return.

- ❖ Creating non-existing projects to support the credibility of the expense and the people who are listed.

- ❖ Having to make sense of the persons name your boss listed on the receipt that was so badly crumpled and stained with the award winning chef's special of the day secret sauce.

- ❖ Trying not to repeat the same people on the expense report even though they would be the ones credible enough to carry off the receipts totaling $300-$400 for drinks and snacks.

- ❖ Keeping a huge box of aspirin in your top right hand drawer for when your boss just so happens to find that last receipt after you've totaled the report for only the one hundredth time.

ROLES ASSISTANTS PLAY

ROLES ASSISTANTS PLAY

COUNSELOR:

The boss comes in on Monday morning looking distraught and sad. You know it probably has something to do with the new guy she's seeing. She looks as if she really needs someone to talk to, but DARN!—you have 2 million things on your "To Do List" (She put 1.9 million of them there herself) but she is your boss and if she's happy then you're happy. 'Cause if she's sad, believe me your day will be pure hell which might turn into a week-long thing. So you knock softly on her door and ask to come in. Once inside you ask how her weekend went while silently praying to yourself that she says everything was great. But that would be too easy. She then of course pouts and begins to tell you how horrible it was. He stood her up, she called his house and another woman answered the phone- the whole shebang! At this point you secretly begin to imagine yourself plotting to kill this guy for not only your boss, but also and more importantly, for you. See, if he didn't create this situation then none of this would be happening but since he did, he deserves to be punished.

Now, back to your boss; you put on your most soothing "DJ" voice while holding her hand in that comforting way, and patiently sit through 2 hours of her self pitying jibber jabber. The more she talks the more everything starts sounding like "Blah, blah, blah". When this happens, you know you've been listening to her a little too long. You finally see some sign of hope in her eyes that she will be alright and you then return to your desk emotionally drained. You're more behind in your work and you know you should expect her to ask you within the next 5 minutes "Where is the memo I asked you for?" Your reply automatically will be, "I'm almost done!" Knowing good and well you haven't even put the date on the memo yet. She then has the nerve to ask you who has called as if you weren't in the office with her for the past two hours.

TRANSLATOR:

You hone this skill by:
Picking up your boss' voice mail messages and trying to figure out what the caller from the cell phone with the really bad static is saying to you, and actually getting it right. By being able to read the half transmitted faintly printed fax that has that very important date and address on it that your boss is desperately waiting on. Trying to make out what her crybaby friends are saying when they call the office all broken up over something like a hangnail.

Your translator skills are most needed when you try to understand what your boss' 2 year old is talking about when he thinks he's saying the world to you. You have this pasted on smile like he's the most adorable thing in the world, but in your mind you're saying "What in the heck are you saying little boy?"

PATHOLOGICAL LIAR:

You cover for your boss when questioned by the big boss on her whereabouts. Her 8:00 a.m. hair appointment is now her mammogram appointment, her nail appointment is now her doctors appointment and her hot 3 hour lunch date with the flavor of the week is now being called a root canal.

REFEREE:

Your boss is mad at her boyfriend, she comes in and announces she is not taking "Bob's" calls. Of course soon as she says this he calls.

- -Hi Sue! Can I speak to Ginger please?

Now Bob is the kindest, sweetest guy she's ever dated (and believe me, you've met every joke she's ever let into her life) and you hate to lie to him.

- No, I'm sorry Bob, but Ginger isn't in yet.
- Are you sure? I just spoke to her on the car phone and she was pulling into the parking structure.
- Really? Well, maybe she's downstairs talking. I'll go take a look.

You put Bob on hold and buzz Ginger in her office.

- WHAT??????????
- Bob's on line 1.
- Tell him I don't want to talk to him.
- Are you sure?
- Yes. I hate him!

- Why don't you just give him a chance?
- I'll take the call but I'm telling him it's over.
- Should I get off the phone?
- No. I want you to be my witness that I'm through with him for good this time.
- Okay. Hold on.

As you put her on hold, you curse yourself for being so stupid. You should have just made up some excuse and told Bob to call back. Now you're in the middle of this mess.

- Bob? I found her. I'm going to conference you in now.
- I told you she was there.
- Ginger? I have Bob on the line.
- Good. Now Sue, let me tell you what he did.
- Wait a minute, how come you get to go first? Let me explain my side of the story.

What ensues is a 30 minute conversation or should I say, shouting match between the two of them with you acting as the referee. Both of them are trying to get you to see their points and both of them sound like idiots.

Now if you think this is bad, what's worse is if they are husband and wife. In that situation if you must pick a side, pick the wife's side, please. See men aren't that petty. If you are a man he'll just think you're a coward, and if you are a woman he'll get over it and chalk it up to women sticking together. But if you are a woman and you pick the husbands side, you'll never hear the end of it. The wife will never forgive you and will forever think you are trying to steal her husband. She will never look at you the same again. Trust me.

BABYSITTER

This happens more often if you are unfortunate enough to work out of your boss' home. She'll be at a meeting; of course she got there late so it's going to take longer to end. It's about 10 'til six and you're packing up your things, you got a hot date, the first one this year. Your boss calls the office:

-Oh great! You're still there.
-Umm. Yeah.
-Look, I need a favor.
-Uh huh.
-Can you watch Precious for me?
-Ummm….
-Great! I'll be home about 9:30 p.m.
-9:30?
-Yes. After the meeting we're going out for cocktails.
-Oh.
-Alright. See you soon.

Now, if the above example only happened once or twice or every blue moon it wouldn't be so bad. But it's normally 2 or 3 times a week. And when you suggest that she may want to look into a professional babysitting service (You've slipped a couple of referrals on her desk) her response is:
-Naw, I don't think I can afford that, plus it's not like I need one that often.

ROLES YOUR BOSS WOULD ASK YOU TO PLAY IF SHE COULD GET AWAY WITH IT

1. CAR WASHER
   I sometimes get the feeling that if it were up to my boss she would ask me to wash her car when the car detailing guy takes too long to come and do it for her.

2. RUNNER
   When we are having really bad weather outside, I begin to notice my boss eyeballing me as if to ask me to brave the hail, sleet and snow in order to pick up her lunch.

3. MAID
   My boss drops big beat me over the head hints as to how dirty and unorganized her house is and that she has no time to clean up due to her work schedule. I can see her now, suggesting Friday is sweats and T-shirt day at the "HOME OFFICE"

4. MASSEUSE

When my boss is in need of a massage, she begins to slouch over with one hand on her hip while trying to reach over to massage her neck with the other hand and tops it off with a sighing moan or two in my direction.

5. EXTERMINATOR

Occasionally we have ants in the office. However, it appears that the only little thing my boss can crush while wearing her new pumps is my ego.

6. BEAUTICIAN

My boss comes into the office almost every day with big bad out-dated hair. As she talks to me she runs her fingers through it and scratches her scalp. She then mentions that her beautician is booked and she doesn't know what to do and how she could just die. I pay her no mind until she walks away looking defeated.

JUST CALL ME MANDO THE MAGNIFICENT

JUST CALL ME MANDO THE MAGNIFICENT

As the day goes on, I am asked to perform a variety of duties, which I never thought were possible to do while on the phone taking a message

- ❖ Take down a dictated message, which is being yelled at me from the other room for a memo that does not go out until maybe tomorrow at the earliest.

- ❖ Greet co-workers as they ignore the fact that I'm on the phone.

- ❖ Get someone on the other line for my boss while I'm still on the first line with the person she is dodging a call from as if they can't hear her voice in the background instructing me on what to do.

- ❖ Recall who was at the premiere of such and such's latest movie and who represents that lead actor, you recall, the one who was only in the movie long enough for you to blink an eye.

❖ Mentally recall the name and phone numbers of the last five people who called around the time of 10:45 a.m. even though it's now 3:30 p.m.

❖ Get that really important person on the line, you know, the one who wasn't important enough to put on speed dial and even if he was on your boss' speed dial, guess what, you would still have to dial him up on your own line and then transfer him to your boss who just can't seem to push that one little speed dial button.

❖ Keep yourself from slapping the person who is tapping you on your shoulder repeatedly only to find out they wanted nothing.

❖ Retrieve the fax out of the fax tray that the caller on the line is asking you about that has been purposely sitting there because you knew she sent it and you were trying to ignore it.

❖ Memorize your boss' social, business, and personal calendar so when asked with whom she's lunching you'll actually have the right answer this time.

❖ Find a way to get your boss coffee, heat up her bagel, slice her fruit and stay on the line with her, even though the kitchen is down the hall and you're not on a cordless.

❖ Get the file out of her file drawer located behind her desk which she is not able to reach because her swivel chair doesn't quite turn all the way in that direction.

YOU KNOW YOU'RE STRESSED WHEN...

YOU KNOW YOU'RE STRESSED WHEN...

You know you are experiencing stress on the job when you begin to see things under a different light:

- ❖ You see the letter opener as a member of the ice pick family.

- ❖ Your desk turns into a shrine covered with relaxation candles, incense, stress relief pills and green tea.

- ❖ You put in an order for a larger and sharper pair of scissors to be delivered ASAP.

- ❖ You make sure your boss' coffee is scalding hot because you want her to burn the same tongue she uses to talk down to you.

- ❖ You take her phone receiver and have the sick guy of the office breath heavily on it few times just for luck.

❖ You purposely check her drinking glass making sure it has as much soap liquid residue as possible, oh and a chipped rim wouldn't hurt either.

❖ That very important package she's been waiting on will be hidden for a few days, or until you feel she's suffered long enough, and then you give it to her. But before you do you remember to beat it on the ground and step on it a few times with dusty shoes to make it look like it's been through the ringer and remove the post marked date. Once this is done, you then rush into her office with a breathless and concerned look as to what the hell happened to this very important package she's been waiting on and why the hell is it just now arriving.

❖ Her bills that were to go out on a certain day will now go out the day after the due date guaranteeing a late charge.

❖ Her significant other just might accidentally be called by another man's name when he calls the office to speak to her.

❖ You RSVP on the same day for the party of the year guaranteeing she will not get in.

❖ Liquid White Out along with glue and heavily scented markers are your new best friends.

❖ You arrive and leave the office exactly on time.

❖ You purposely dress warmly as you "accidentally" adjust the office thermostat to the lowest temperature possible.

❖ You bring your lunch to work faithfully in order to avoid her asking you to pick-up lunch for her while you're out. Her request is a conscious one because she's aware that she's cutting into your lunch, but she refuses to extend you any extra time.

❖ You begin to drop big hints that you are no longer single which means don't ask me to come in early, nor stay late and babysitting her brat is out of the question.

❖ For those of us without caller I.D. at home, we allow all calls to go directly to voice mail in case it's the boss. Once we've retrieved the voice mail message and learned that in fact it was the boss who had the nerve to call you at home, we thank our lucky stars for coming up with that brilliant plan.

❖ You welcome a severe case of the flu just so you can exercise your right as a team player by going into work and spreading your germs.

❖ When ordering office supplies you tend to favor the ones that can double as a weapon, i.e., scissors, letter openers, hole punchers, pointers, glass paper weights, giant glass coffee mugs, metal rulers, staple removers, brass desk lamps, etc…

YOU KNOW YOU'RE A CHEESY ASSISTANT WHEN...

YOU KNOW YOU'RE A CHEESY ASSISTANT WHEN...

❖ Your boss gives you an urgent package to mail and you find it 2 days later on the back seat of your car.

❖ You have to ask your boss 5 times to repeat the last 6 words of a 4 sentence paragraph he's dictating to you.

❖ You take so long to type a report, your boss volunteers to do it herself.

❖ You know every cute guy in the office but can't seem to recall the complicated name of the female receptionist down the hall. You know: Jane.

❖ You wait until you have 5 minutes left on your lunch break to take care of that important errand you needed to run for your boss.

❖ Every member of the maintenance staff knows you by name because you keep breaking stuff.

❖ You accidentally fax classified information to a competitor.

❖ When your boss calls you from the car asking for so and so's number you immediately put her on hold and run to the "Perfect Assistant" to get the number. You jump back on the line with your boss and give her the number that you should have had in your rolodex.

❖ Instead of typing directions for your boss to get to his movie shoot you hand write them. Because you're lazy you use initials. And because you write like a pre-schooler, your second "S" looks like a "5" So your boss ends up driving down the 55 freeway lost and confused when he was supposed to be taking highway 5S(South).

OOPS

Instead of taking the time to ask a caller to spell their difficult sounding name (you are too embarrassed to ask) you just sound it out and creatively come up with what you assume is the correct spelling. Then you give the message to your boss and forget all about it. That is, until your boss comes screaming out of her office two weeks later, because she sent him a note thanking him for some wonderful deed and on the note she spelled his name exactly the way you wrote it- WRONG.

PROBLEM...SOLUTION

PROBLEM...SOLUTION

PROBLEM: Okay, someone calls for your boss and you give her the message. She says okay and that's it. Then about an hour later she says, "Okay, what's so and so's number again? I want to call her back." Of course by now you not only forgot where you put the message, but when you find it, you look and realize that you forgot to get their number.

SOLUTION: So you calmly tell your boss, "Hold on a second, I have another call". You put her on hold; quickly call someone else who you believe may have the number. She doesn't. She tells you to try information. Good Idea! You swiftly call information praying you at least have the right city. God blesses you with the number. You jump back on the phone with your boss trying not to breathe too hard. You say, "okay, I have the number right here. Are you ready?" (Note: this only works if your boss calls you on the phone. Face to face is a whole different story.)

PROBLEM: When at 4:30 your boss asks you to call her friend and say she'll be 15 minutes late and you don't think about it until 5:15.

SOLUTION: By this time she's already there. So when you talk to your boss, just tell her you kept trying to reach her friend but you just couldn't get through. "Maybe there's something wrong with her phone."

PROBLEM: You want to take an extended lunch break without your boss finding out.

SOLUTION: You take the last phone call before you leave at 1:00 p.m. but on the phone log you log the time of the call to be 1:25 p.m. Always remember to beat your boss back to the office in order to pick up her voice mail messages in case some idiot called in between 1:00 and 1:25 p.m.

PROBLEM: When your boss calls you from her cell phone with major static on the line only to give you a horrendous list of things she wants you to do that you don't care to do.

SOLUTION: You conveniently take advantage of the bad static situation. First, inform her that can barely hear her. Second, constantly ask her to repeat herself even though you heard her the first time. Next, you lower your voice to a faint whisper and crumple paper near the receiver in order to create fake static. Last, but not least, you hang up, securing that you don't have to do the list from hell.

MISTAKES ASSISTANTS MAKE...

MISTAKES ASSISTANTS MAKE...

SPECIAL SKILL OR TALENTS:
Whatever you do, do not let your boss know that you have a special talent or abilities. Some may think it would be beneficial to inform their boss of all the different skills they have mastered. (Of course on your resume and in your initial interview you want to come off as the master of all, but everyone's supposed to try and make that first impression.) But it is the fool who after 2 months working on the job is still bringing her boss decorative cakes and cookies, knitted sweaters, nifty ceramic originally designed invitations made by the one legged, half blind lady in a third world country and other homemade things. Why do you ask? Because believe me, this dummy will be booked up every weekend until she's 50; doing this and that for her boss' relatives and friends. Some may feel that at least they are getting their foot in the door, you know, future customers in case they want to open their own business one day. But it doesn't work that way. Her boss

and her cheap friends will continue to use her up until she's all dried up and out of ideas and leaves to find another job. Then they'll wait patiently 'til the next one of them hires another dummy assistant and the cycle begins again.

THE DIARY PART II
(THE VETERAN)

THE DIARY PART II (THE VETERAN)

This morning is my first day back at work after calling in sick knowing good and well I spent the entire day shopping with my sister who supports anyone who calls in sick for whatever reason. It's now a new day and I'm hoping all will go well for me in the office. As usual I'm running late and as I walk in the office I can hear the phone ringing off the hook. I think to myself, what fool is calling this early in the morning and how dare they call me before I even take a seat and settle in.

I snatch up the phone as I smother my attitude. The person hangs up in my face. After a few million swear words, I blow off the hang up call. Two minutes later three of seven lines decide to ring all at once. Like the veteran assistant that I am, I clear the first two calls with ease. The third call though is the big boss looking for my boss. Of course my "kiss the big boss' butt" personality instantly turns on. I schmooze for a quick second and lie to him about my boss having an early, outside meeting. He buys it and proceeds to ask me about issues he discussed with my boss as if I have the slightest idea about what he's talking about. I then have to admit in a very sweet tone that I have no recollection of what he's talking about as his voice sounds like he's saying, "Please remind me why you're working for the company". The conversation then ends very swiftly after that.

As I enter my office and look at the mess I left on my desk from last Friday I begin to realize that my organized chaos isn't as organized as I left it. My immediate thought is that the temp had something to do with this. It's not like I can call her and yell at her for not returning my rolodex cards to the rolodex, but just the thought of me calling her and being really anal about something like that made me put a corner smile on my face.

My eyes then lock onto this huge box on my desk that says "TRANSCRIBER" on it.

TRANSCRIBER. When this thing arrived last week all I thought was this can only mean one thing- more work for me. "Laura! I have a letter I want done. Could you grab the TRANSCRIBER and come here please?" "Laura! I have a memo that I want you to do. Could you grab the TRANSCRIBER?" "Laura, I have a thought. Could you...." Get the picture? My first thought was to run down to the corner store and purchase a mini screwdriver to tinker with it. My next thought was the company would only replace it with another one and so on and so on. Rage coats my fluffy body as I realized there's nothing I could do about the situation but accept it and move on. I hated the feeling of defeat. Five days have passed and my boss has not even recorded one single thing on the TRANSCRIBER from hell. Can you say "Amen"? Still, I keep it in open view so she can think that I'm interested in it. It's funny, now that I think about it, I realize that I subconsciously placed the TRANSCRIBER right above the trash can as if I was waiting for it to *accidentally* fall in. I swear, things that are done subconsciously hold a lot of meaning.

It's now break time and my co-worker and another assistant from another department and I are all in my boss' office, laughing it up while she's still out at her "meetings." All of a sudden, out of nowhere the other assistant's boss comes over with a look as if she could do a "Three Stooges" slap on all of our faces. She proceeds to ask what's so funny and then says we're being too loud as she pulls the door shut from the outside, and drags her assistant along with her. "If this brat was not the boss' daughter I would kick her in the teeth", I thought to myself. I look at my other co-worker like "did what just happened, really happen?" From this point on, she will be on my hate list. I feel bad for her assistant because I know something will be said to her but that's between her and "Little Ms. I'll-tell-my-daddy."

My boss has breezed in and is exhausted so decides to take a shopping break. Out the door she goes. I give it one full minute before the first call comes in. nly be my boss, who by the way just left only sixty seconds ago. I quickly snatch up the phone and answer in my professional manner while camouflaging my "I-know-it's-you-and-why-couldn't-you-have-told-me-this-before-you-left" voice. My boss proceeds to give me a list of "To do's" as if it wasn't already written on the three page "To Do" letterhead on my desk. I humor both her and myself and reply "let me grab a pen and paper". While my boss continues to talk I hear static on the line assuming she's going through a tunnel. Well, needless to say, I cease the opportunity to snatch a few pieces of paper and crumple it by the phone as if to let her know the static is really bad and that we are breaking up. She continues to talk as if our reception is clear on both ends and then I follow up on the crumpling of the paper by dropping my voice to a whisper type level while fading away. She finally gets the message and says she will call me back in a few minutes. If that ploy would have failed I would have resorted to Plan "B", which was to remind her that we are breaking up, followed by "I can't hear you, your words are choppy", ending with a polite hang up in her face.

Now that I'm finally off the phone I glance at my "To Do" list noticing something I really hate to do which is the dreaded expense report. My jaws drop at the total dollar amount of the meal receipts. Three of them together are equivalent to my rent. What the hell are they serving at those restaurants, a hot plate of diamond rings smothered in a fur coat, dipped in platinum, sprinkled with two round trip tickets to a four star resort? I suck it up and start the expense report.

The phone rings and I look over at it as if I could just rip it out of the wall and throw it under a speeding car. I politely answer it only to find out it's her "rude" friend. This woman talks at the speed of light and then wants me to dictate back to her what she just said. My first thought is "HELLO?" weren't you paying attention?" I pause for a minute, count to 10 and dictate it to her and finally the phone conversation ends with her rude butt saying "Very good". This is one person I'd better not ever catch out after hours.

I'm now back to the expense report from hell. I'll never figure out how anyone can eat a full breakfast, lunch and fifty course dinners almost every single day and wonder why they can't lose weight. As soon as that thought leaves my mind the phone rings again, but this time it's her "Wanna-Be, I'm-God's-Gift-to-Women" loser friend. To annoy him, I make it a point to ask whose calling, knowing good and well it's his sorry behind. He always calls and occasionally my boss might decide to return his call. Some people just don't get it. We end the conversation with the usual "I'll give her the message" while silently saying under my breath the famous five letter word, "Loser".

The phone rings again and it's my boss' "crybaby" friend who doesn't have a man. Let's see, could the reason for that be that she spends all of her time calling and crying to my boss over not having a man? Oh well, maybe one day she'll find someone. I almost feel like going out and building her one.

Earlier this week we finally moved into our new offices. I'm so happy because now I have access to real office supplies, fax machine, copier, etc… In the past when I had these luxuries I took them for granted not knowing one day I could be without them. Now I know how to appreciate things in the office like "Spell Check". I had been working on a computer without my lovely "Spell Check" and I almost died. The tiniest of words for some reason, I was misspelling. I don't know if it was a mental thing because I knew I didn't have "Spell Check" that all of a sudden I started spelling words wrong. I spelled "The" with a "4"; it looked like "Th4". Thank God I had a dictionary and the patience to proofread my work or else I would have looked like Queen Idiot of the office. I'm so glad that I'm now back on a fully loaded computer along with my soul mate, A.K.A. "Spell Check".

My boss finally comes back to the office her usual one-hour late which I'm hoping will move up to two. She greets me in a very pleasant tone and asks me to get her a cup of coffee, which I'm more than happy to do. Anything that will get me away from my area and her eagle eye is okay by me. I return with her coffee only to have her point out to me that she now has a voicemail message and that I should check it. The key word in that sentence is <u>now</u> which implies that there wasn't a message earlier. She tells me to check the message and my first thought was "why don't you check your own message?" followed by "well, she is the boss and it is part of my job description." As I am checking the message the phone rings. Instead of her picking up her line, she tells me to answer it. I hang up from checking the message in order to answer her phone. As I pick it up I hear her in the background as she picks it up along with me but she doesn't say anything until she recognizes the caller's voice and then she yells out to me that she's got it as if that wasn't obvious.

I return to checking her message only to find out it's her annoying-voice mother who calls every ten minutes to make sure everything is okay. Her mother proceeds to leave a message long enough to cut a box set collection. Three pages later, I'm finally done taking the message. My boss' one o'clock calls to suggest a lunch location which we agree upon. My boss then asks me to call to find out where the restaurant is located and to make reservations. I assume my boss doesn't know where the restaurant is located and that is why she asked me to call and get the address. I go the extra mile and even get the directions for her. Five minutes later her one o'clock calls me back and asks for the address and directions of the restaurant she herself suggested. At this moment I become concerned with the thought that my boss is having lunch with an undercover idiot. I pause and give the dummy the information she needs. Also I ponder, why she would ask me this info and not her assistant. I mean, is she paying her assistant to sit on his or her butt while an outside assistant does all the work? I snap out of it and give her the address and directions to the best of my knowledge based on where her office is located. She then tells me that she will not be leaving from her office, but from her 12 o'clock nail appointment on the other side of the hill. I think to myself, "Now is that my problem, do I look like Mrs. Thomas Guide"? She then goes on to say that she will find it somehow and I think to myself "and if you don't, too bad".

It's now time for my boss to leave for her lunch and I secretly do a "she's leaving the office dance" in my head as I wish her a good lunch. I'm now exhausted from the morning madness and it's time for me to take my lunch. I know I want to lunch with someone in the office, but I'm not sure who to ask. I debate whether I should take the office nerd who will quietly sit there and listen to me while I run my big mouth, or should I lunch with the office busybody? I choose the office nerd because I can always depend on this person to maintain my confidence as I rant and rave about everyone else. The office nerd is that one person you can curse to, tell your wild weekend adventures to, and gossip to. This person is your one true ally in the work place. Lunch seems to go by so fast with him because he finds just about anything you say to him funny and he never corrects you. You feel like you are on top of the world with this person because he allows you the freedom to talk with no judgment. I like that. When I think about it, this person is truly a great person and friend. Not because he doesn't pass judgment on me but because there is a sense of trust which is a rarity in the workplace.

Oh man. I hear my boss' keys rattle in the door and I poise my entire body with that upright-focused-busy look on my face. I greet her as I sense she's in a great mood. I love it when my boss is in her great moods. This is when I can practically commit murder and she would cover for me. She tends to want to offer to buy me lunch, or let me leave early for the day. She only has to ask me once about the leaving early part. Hell, as soon as I hear the first two words "do you..." I have already agreed to it. For all I know she could probably be asking me "do you want to stay late" and I, being so quick to answer, agreed to it like a fool.

Well, the day is about to end and I am finally able to see the cherry wood face of my desk as opposed to a sea of memos and unsorted mail. I've returned to my cubical, the one with the great view. I stop and look around. I love my cubical. I have pictures of my family, friends, greeting cards, and little trinkets my boss was thoughtful enough to bring back from her out-of-town trips. I know I complain about my boss, but she is truly a very kind hearted person. She keeps me in the loop about everything. She is informative, smart, patient, likeable, strong, aggressive, thorough, and generous. When I have a bad day, I remind myself that I would not have a job if it were not for her.

Well enough of that crazy talk. It's quitting time. I say goodbye to my desk, telephone, computer and the transcriber and head towards the door. It's been an exciting day and believe it or not I will be ready to start all over again tomorrow.

I know I often get frustrated and disgusted by some of the things my boss does but I guess that's par for the course. There will be days when she irritates me so much I will scream. Then there will be days when I mess up so badly I will just want to fire myself and save her the trouble.

Remembering that there will be both good times and bad times helps me stay in this position, day after day after day because someday I know I'll reach my goal. I mean I won't be an assistant forever right?

QUOTES

Some may believe that we are just bitter assistants whom from the looks of things are so cheesy and lazy that we make an easy job seem hard. Well we've got news for you. We've asked several other top notch assistants (who like ourselves know better than to reveal their true identities) to express their feelings regarding this job.
Here's what they said:
1. "If she (my boss) would just do what she's supposed to do instead of interrupting what I'm trying to do, to tell me to do something she could have done herself, then I could get something done!"
2. "When I die, I am sure that at my funeral I will be in my casket and as they lower me into the ground I'll hear a knock and it'll be my boss saying, "Hey there's just one more thing I need you to do!"
3. "I was working with a guy and I was his assistant. One day I looked up and saw my face in the mirror and I thought I say my mother's mother. I could not believe how much I had aged working for him."

EPILOGUE

EPILOGUE

Now, some of you might be thinking that if being an assistant is this hard or frustrating, why do you do it? TO PAY THE BILLS DARN IT!!! Well, that's actually just one of the reasons. Some people do it as a means to an end. You know, trying to climb up that corporate ladder. So if that's the case then most of the bosses out there were once sitting in that lowly little chair outside too. So you'd think they'd know better. But that's how people are, always forgetting where they came from. But honestly one of the main reasons someone becomes an assistant is because they are extremely organized, efficient and professional and want to use their God given talents to assist someone else in creating or completing work that's worthwhile. To all you bosses out there. Do us a favor. Take a little time to treat your assistant like an assistant, not a slave and maybe you'll get better results from them. And to all you assistants- keep on fighting the good fight. Because we all know, behind every great boss, there's an assistant, standing in his shadow, ready to strangle him.

PennyLee

www.ingramcontent.com/pod-product-compliance
Lightning Source LLC
Chambersburg PA
CBHW051708040426
42446CB00008B/785